When All My Disappointments Came At Once

For Misha :-)

November 6 2012 Toronto

When All My Disappointments Came At Once

with great love —

Todd Swift

& glad to see you again!

with enjoyment of your books... and best,

Todd

Copyright © 2012 Todd Swift
All rights reserved

Tightrope Books
17 Greyton Crescent
Toronto, Ontario. M6E 2G1
www.tightropebooks.com

Edited by Catherine Graham
Typesetting by Dawn Kresan
Cover design by David Bigham
Cover art by Stewart MacFarlane
http://www.stewartmacfarlane.com/

Printed and bound in Canada

We thank the Canada Council for the Arts and the Ontario Arts Council for their support of our publishing program.

Canada Council for the Arts   Conseil des Arts du Canada

ONTARIO ARTS COUNCIL
CONSEIL DES ARTS DE L'ONTARIO

Library and Archives Canada Cataloguing in Publication

Swift, Todd, 1966–
    When all my disappointments came at once / Todd Swift.

Poems.
ISBN 978-1-926639-45-1

    I. TITLE.

PS8587.W5W44 2012   C811'.54   C2012-901804-X

To my wife Sara & my godson Alex

The highest criticism is the record of one's own soul

　—Oscar Wilde

I said to my soul, be still, and wait without hope

　—T.S. Eliot

Then, swift behind the stage, my third disguise:
Hard-helmeted, and blind, and indolent,
Learned on bells and the behavior of grass,
The playboy with the famous instrument,
The spinster with an attic of old brass

　—Terence Tiller

Table of Contents

Listening In   9
The Shelf   10
On Reading Martin Mooney   13
The land I'd wish to describe   14
In Memory of F.T. Prince   15
Michael Kohlhaas   18
Hedda Gabler   21
Jean Talon, Intendant of New France, To the King (1666)   23
Amirs of the House of Rashid   25
I Think of Delmore Schwartz, Beside My Sleeping Love   28
After Terence Tiller   31
On The Sublime   32
God has left us like a girl   33
August 1982, Lac Bridgen   34
Seven Good Fridays   35
My 43rd Year   40
St Peter and St Paul   41
October ray   43
On Television   45
New Country   46
Song in a Time of Inflation   47
Shop-Worn   49
The Farmer's Wife   50
Azoospermia   51
After riding the escalator back   53
When all my disappointments came at once   55
Fertility   56
Sonnet   57
Our Children   58
St Lambert   59
The Runner   60

Slieve Donard 61
'Down from St John's Wood' 63
September's End 64
Hope, Maida Vale 65
Near St Ives 66
Fire Killed The Sculptor As She Worked 67
The Snow Child 68
Slieve Donard II 69
A Walk with Sara In September 71
Old Master 73
Improbable August 74
Pont D'Avignon 75
Winter Storm Lothar 76
The Safe Years 77
For Sara 79
Start Again 80
Lines Composed On The Poet's Sterility 83
Hunting Party 84
After a First Line by David Lehman 85
Esophagitis 86
Love Or Poetry 87
London Reflux 88
Rain 89
Water in a Lakeland Vale 90
Request 91
The Ailment 92

Author Biography 95
Acknowledgements 97
Praise for Todd Swift 101

Listening In

Things are what kings hold—and let go of, once,
Learning too late that the nothing outside belongs
To the nothingness sighing in our blood, and will

Connect to it, as a burglar will drill through
Steel locks and busy tumblers, to our blood.
We sense the vibrancy of loss is violins—

A surgery wild with last-minute cutting, a tuning
Up of instruments and mastery—this universe
Has a body like a dancer, a mind like a jackal.

The Shelf

I had come to the place,
Where, hearing talk of it,
One thinks never to reach:
The past-clever home
For poets, when, inkhorn
Dry, their plain pure language
Has run out, like some
Battered car in Texas,
Miles and miles from gas,
Ironic in the midst of all
The diving pens into the soil,
Those upstart, down-turning
Peckers that dive for oil,
And dot the desert like a rash;
Judging by such an arid
Moonscape as a base to write,
One leans on the hood, chews
A 'pick and spits, to think
On all the vast wide space
Bequeathed to the mind,
To imagine as full of something
Else: the roaming creatures
That writing finds. A lodestone
Or lone star sort of state, depending—
But basically, blank as a cheque
From a friend who has up and died,
So you might scrawl in some line
Pretending to be them, to cash in,
But can't—your style your own
Or, following on Seneca, refined.
What died to make words ring?
I load my ore with outlandish

Clutter, not to bring the steer in
To brand, or land the walloping
Salmon to the shore, but to sing
A score that has no meaning other than
Artifice or authenticity: both begin
In someone (or automaton) pretending
To compose by laying words on end,
An endless track from sea to sea,
On which all industry and commerce
Depend. I don't claim to be Jesse
James, or the King James version, either,
Liable to halt the engine as it sails
Across the waves of prairie, to offload
The golden insight in the big black vault.
The fault is in the chug-chug procession
Of creation, which begins to cease,
Like biological conditions of the specimen;
Organic? Didn't mean to be, believe
In quite the reverse, creation less Darwinian,
The finger-zapped instanter blast of a God
Making all everything ever at once,
Which, when written (said) sounds false,
Perhaps the reason writing is dangerous:
By putting down the line one shows
Precisely the ignorance by which one knows
What isn't true or cannot be said, what
Thoughts, before they happened, were
Not even oozing from the oil of the head.
So there's the theme I haven't had:
Two summers since I tended to my Dad,
Dying, as all do, and how mourning fed
A kind of released grandeur from my tongue;

As when I wanted poetry, when young;
Now, having stopped my sorrow
As one does, in time, I have also found
No more reason to need to rhyme;
It is the ending of the need begins
The play—the spooling out of the spider's
Fibre strong as caution but light as day—
Enwebbed, one writes, or then is written on,
And nothing placed into the midst belongs
To evidence or witness stand—floats free—
Or hopes to, in sticky search of locking-in
The wriggling at the pit of poetry—
A smallest beast, to suck dry of its blood,
An ending better than the start is good.

On Reading Martin Mooney

It's climbed to, then taken down—
let's say it is a sun-fed sphere—
to tangle with an earthy palate—
but the orchard in which making occurs
is rare, and self-claimed—
no other hand can lift the ladder
or bring the body to the branch required.

No, it's often ignored,
how the act is squired
with great care, even a noble attention—
spoiled because some are stolen
effortlessly—by talent or conceit—
to counterfeit the seat of love
as that of reason
when, in or out of season, the labour
in the high yard where the fruit bestows
its gift is more difficult than thought.

To climb doesn't always yield
an abundant basket on its own;
still, plenty does happen—
a verbal or a tropic outcome—
from such an uplifting *despite*.

The land I'd wish to describe

Contains beasts more delightful than art itself;
They curl about the foliage like smart imps
And pelt us both with bold fruit, chattering

Like those who prefer celebrity to the genuine.
Inside this jungle we'd come to a shelf
On which the heads of chieftains had lain;

When sacrificed, they fell like blossoms in a stream.
Touch the cold worn grooves of this ancient thing.
Here is how the savages anoint their king.

How fortunate we are to live elsewhere
Among a people always temperate and wise
Who have no laws able to boil their blood alive,

Who have no faith to make them bring down a knife.
Placid and good, our island is, unlike this place
Drawn for your pleasure; unable to spread

Or cause upheaval, really, in the vibrant world,
In which the riches that are wanted can be seen
And, as if at market on a table, taken.

In Memory of F.T. Prince

'Because to love is terrible we prefer/The freedom of our crimes' – from an early published version of 'Soldiers Bathing', F.T. Prince, Captain, M.E.F. (British)

Desire ages, ages hardly at all,
Edges, like those of a book,
Curled at the beach, where waves,
Sent by the summer, brush

The salt away, finely-combed,
And it is homosexual love
That holds us in its palm,
That cuts and dries the hair

We both wore, like uniforms,
That day that was a decade,
Though neither of us found a bed
That could be so cleanly made;

For now, married, on continents
Split as if in some biblical debate,
We have shelved those dreamy
Acts of early indiscipline,

Where, cock from trousers,
Cock in hand, we edged, together
To a cliff, a Christian form
Of final decision, in the Italian sand,

But stepped away from intercourse,
Or love, decided that, as men,
Our hearts belonged to those
Who could tend it otherwise, and so,

Packed up our bathing suits,
And wore trim expressions
Home, at dawn, dressed, like wounds
More deeply in blood-lies.

Words have a purpose if no meaning
Beyond shorelines where they crash,
Which is to deface emotion
With communication, in a style

That drowns the jungle wholesale,
And no ark or personality can swim
Free of its deciding glamour
And deceptive fluidity: so smile,

And say, it was not love that drove
Our Damascene caresses to a cross,
Upon which loss lay openly, but
Desire suffered in its private language—

No, it was decorum, or fear of
Impropriety—simply petty feeling,
Feeling inadequate to emotionality—
But those who nailed the arm of God

Into the wood were strong enough
To withstand hardier cruelty,
And played at the weeping feet,
Just as the artists, unknown mostly

Except for the names of school
Or master, too, commanded passion
To an ordering, pictorial and strange,
Of such derangements of the body

As we could never have drawn
From our quivers to disarrow, true—
So saying, even being, overcome
Is not the terrible action it appears—

No, it is the naïve aversion to it,
Slowly accruing to regret, by year,
That marks the one, who, like Cain,
Enters a town each time as someone

Immediately despised, narrow, pained,
Leaving the districts with stones
For signs the boys follow out with
On the path; love's release is betraying,

Even as it holds back confession
To end as marble, a certain epitaph.

Michael Kohlhaas

after Kleist

First they starved my two black horses;
Then they beat my loyal stable hand
So that now he coughs up blood; he will
Never recover. That would have been enough
To test most good men. My faithful wife
Was struck in the chest on her way
To petition on my behalf. She died
Three days later at my side. That's when
I sold my home, my business, sent the children
Away, over the border, to be safe. I gathered
The few men who could be trusted,
Who knew me, knew I was a just employer.
They too thirsted for vengeance.

We arrived at his castle at night, killed
The first two men we met, quickly.
I whipped a stable boy within an inch
Of his life; we scoured the place. Wives
And children were pitched out of windows
Like excrement. Knights bowed
For forgiveness as if I were the Lord.
I was not the Lord of Mercy, this night.
We lopped heads off like children
Taking the flowers from a field. I waded
In blood, a man fording a shallow stream
To cut a journey short. I lost no man
And turned the Junker castle into a waste of stone,
A field that could not be ploughed. Now
His toll gate was just a dead tree cindered.
I taught these bastards in the language
They spoke, what pain is.

That was only the beginning. Good murder
Is its own calling card. I nailed up warnings—
For the enemy I most wanted had fled
To a nunnery, to hide behind God's skirts.
I would have bloodied that white linen
But when we arrived, a hungry mob of thirteen
Killers with a cause, he was gone ahead,
To Wittenberg. Wittenberg should have prayed
That instead the Black Death had knocked
On their good gates. My men, unknown, blessed
Like cats on silent paws, brought unexpected flames
In the name of Kohlhaas in the night, nineteen
Buildings gone, including a school, two churches.
I nailed up a new warning—give me the bastard.

They did not relent. Second night and more men
Slipped in, fires like sores on a plague victim
Erupted, the whole town danced to the fire,
Trying to find enough water. Look in my eyes
For water. I had wept that ocean dry. Give me
My man. Not so. The third night, the town bells
Rang like every virgin married at once;
Dawn brought groom and bride to their ashen senses;
The timbers and foundations blistered.

What kind of world can men build for each other
If a good man who makes an effort is turned aside
Simply because of nepotism?
High places with no room for honest men encourage
Conversion to a new faith. Mine calls for heresy:
If they won't give me satisfaction, by Christ, I'll nail it out

Skull by skull myself. They sent two armies against me—
But my mob had grown to a hundred like a pestilence.
We took them as they sought to meet, interrupting
Their wedding night by slipping between their own force.
They wept at our love of murder. We knocked them down.

Now that got attention from Martin Luther.
He called me damned, said I should stop. That gave me
Pause. He was a good man, who spoke to our God.
So I dressed in new clothes, under cover of the night
Came to him then, unawares as he scrawled words
Against the Pope, his own war. I begged to confess
And receive the bread and blood of Christ. Luther's
Moral maidenhead resisted my simple thrusts,
I was turned back from that door. He vowed safe passage
If I'd demob. If the army of justice was just dispersed
They would come to control the situation again.

No strongman is more deadly than the disease of an idea
Incubated in the skulls of men, lice in the bed sheets.
Trusting the man, I left, broke the mob, took myself to Dresden
To seek fair repayment in the courts. Half the mob
Like a broken tooth festered in the mouth of the country,
Raped and burnt, a lingering faggot after the fire was out.
They blamed me, and court intrigue and the inherent evil
Of men who love their friends more than the truth,
Sentenced me to die. Not before the black horses, fed
Up to their original rude health, were brought before me.
As I was killed a crowd rushed forward to touch blood.
My good sons were knighted. Their bloodline runs on.

Hedda Gabler

This white wide luxury
Like Venice green water
Lapping at sinking
Places where men
Planning voyages
Circled globe-painted
Floors, and nothing
Inside is good
And nothing outside is
Good enough
A bullet reflects, refracts,
Bloodies like blush,
What is the cosmetic
Gap or gape twixt
Trigger and kiss,
Red is a hole marked
Mind goes, mind is
A house on loan,
Blood banks on this,
Blood loses on less,
The supple market
Of my flesh is lively
In fashioned suits,
Unbuttoning to breastbone
Judges and scholars lick
Only skin, which is flat,
Cold and rips open,
Tears away, label as label,
Permitting anything,
Expressing what is owned;
This shot to me
Says me, says more or less

Beyond saying, says bye,
Says high, says beyond
The exposed sky, a bird
Crushes its brain on glass,
Perceiving what is clear
To be further emptiness
In which to extend wings,
Instead surface declines
To allow, holds, breaks,
And the crackhole shines
With multiple lines, born
From one finger
Saying Hi, saying Now,
Making the future
Spare study for nowhere.

Jean Talon, Intendant of New France, To the King (1666)

Majesty, may this arrive, after months of turmoil
Carried by vassals chafed by violence yet calm
As their tilting little world of wood falls to rise
Bearing them like a nation on uneven histories
Of current and wave, spume and leviathan,
Astounded by dolphin and shark, salt-burnt and wise,
And find you smooth, perfumed, without grief
Or indigestion: vigorous among your scented court.

I write as chief Seigneur, your ever-loyal habitant,
Petitioning for a thing smaller than a flea in rice
Or a bead of sweat amid the corn. August is here,
Chill oblivion of unenviable winter barely run off
So now is the time of white-hot riot and gold growth.
Your lands on the South Shore are pitilessly pelted
With sun that might be melted ingots thrown down
As from the walls of a horde-besieged Avignon

Upon my bald and chapped skull, leather-clad, a ball
The indecently feathered savages might kick for fun.
It is hot—this land runs to extremes like a slattern
On Calvados; we cannot control our slap-happy men
Who have no time to sow seeds not of their own making,
Who would rather gallivant in the scrub and hunt beaver.
I have ten thousand acres of rich fertile land by a river
Wilder, wider and more supreme than the Ganges—

And no one to plant a bean or rip a carrot from the soil.
Majesty, with all my sprightly genius to serve and toil
Yet I am incapable as one mere mortal (though blessed)
To do what must be done, and flourish in this upheaval
Of weather, murder, and sadly-ignorant oblivion, Quebec.

Implore is too weak an expression for what follows—
We need farmers, not rat-trappers, rapscallions, thugs,
Bird-stranglers, or jugglers. We need good wives

To come like sweet blessings in this hazardous limbo,
That feels daily as if there were no Christ, no Laws—
To lie with us in the nights, help us recall the words
We once spoke lightly in our cities and towns
In the human climate of our birthplace. Dispatch ships
Immediately, if you will, otherwise, I shall observe
In a year's turn of the wheel a thousand acres
First of helpless snow then meaningless grass.

Amirs of the House of Rashid

Pull closed the tent and light the lamp;
Outside the sand is wild as time
And goes about the world as if at last
The maker at the first had been tamed

By a later, lesser, angrier blast—
And now, brought low before the lowest
Was found unworthy by its own creation
And sent out to a crowd to be torn apart.

The heart of the night is terrified—
Only this thin flap, these cords, hold
A whirling torment of wind at bay
So we two might sit here in this calm

To drink of the bean and bow, to say
Old truths in tender new ways, beside
The Book of Prophecies we have by heart—
Written into the silk threads of our souls.

For each student of the night is dressed
In robes lined with deeper light,
Tailored with a fearless hand a thousandfold
More assured than ours, which, when it sews,

Pricks skin to bleed or is too narrow, tight
Or loose with pulling all the fabric right.
So: against this rabble of the outer storm
Here in my paradise-cell, too warm or dim

To serve as any model to fit a heaven on,
What brings you in across twelve dunes my son—
Water-drained, fig-denied, burnt of the sun?
You come to declare a war or fend off

A question or request, to pronounce a law
Or buy a wife or camel or claim new powers—
Or perhaps to take a cup in silence an hour
With your uncle who has lately lost a brother

To share in this threatened space remembrance
Of your unwise, heady father, who led
His groundless campaign against that tribe
Had done us no harm nor intended any.

All sweet injuries imagined were repaid
With bitter blows in a desert flood
Of curved swords raining from riders.
Nod, be quiet, hold out your hand. See,

The lines that move on your palm do so alone.
Your caravan has broken and been lost.
Singular, you struggle to locate a line,
To stumble across a holy furnace to a well.

Drink of your heart, though its pain
Not be balm. Cool your mind's sword, until
It be sheathed. Be regained. At home.
Be at home in your emotions, guided back

Safely, to open that first book we each carry within—
Printed, as I said, with love, not desire
Or madness for revenge. I grant you your peace
For you to fully command. Your companions will have

Rest and time here for the coming days
Until this mindful air has blown itself out.
Then, go back to your people and claim defeat.
For me, it is time to see the clean stars. Wrapped

With care, staying in a modest position
I can withstand the eternal moment's rage
For enough of loud war in an hour's tumult
To make this best journey to be starlit, blessed.

I Think of Delmore Schwartz, Beside My Sleeping Love

Romantic, an American lyric
Pitched to Plato, past a sleeping blonde
By my side (Frisch's *Stiller* slipped

From her hand like a hypodermic)—
As birdsong dictates a serious letter
Calling out for madness and History
To meet underground, Spring's

Union in the grave, that breaks
When love's excess proves rhetoric
Can be poetry before it persuades.

Beauty read Freud and smoked cigarettes,
Was smart, milk came in bottles, those vessels
Rattled, and genocide was still
Locked in the razor of one ill heart.

The complex mode puts leaves on trees
And Summer is a good idea of the mind
Long before ever it was experience—

For we imagine knowledge to be good
And sure, even though, as Eden's children
Mostly what we knew was unconfined—
Our syntax slipped away from land,

Our rocking beds sailed on moonlight
The frost of sky our beaconing horizon.
Awake ghost voyager now, who sank

In the unmoored mind's Mariana,
Unrafted, swollen with brain-rot,
Wracks of passion—unable to know friend
Or pirate in the shadow of shadow.

The sublime may call for clarity
But is often served by vague men who doom
Their jutting prows to strike odd reefs,

Unroofed by calm lingo and straighter goals.
Only in subtle bays or surface shoals
Do tides or pools destroy; not in desert rooms;
The gloom is the sea spray breaking in.

So were your self-made cuts to brow
Of mad projections (of madder maps) both slight
Surface and submarine profound too—sufficient

To render sinking thoughts and feelings
Mirroring out emotion, casting a beam to blind—
Blindness not bestowing wisdom but poison
To fog the clown, whose mask of white pain

Conveys words for pain as well; mascara on skin
That goes to the roots subcutaneous and beyond.
To die alone is to contain a sorrow blossoming

Before sane Spring arrives, to know disorder
Thriving like a bulb bled in shaken ground,
Still the ground the only self that one can own,
So one's garden is infested with an early frost even

In the middle of a bright-seeming normal sun.
A renaissance as rain bows down the cherry tree,
As men cough in thin hallways before they frown

To click at keys that lead them on through frail doors
To places of walls, pale carpets and burns on floors
That speak of beige traffic, and fisticuffs in closets.
To fail is obscure—it means one first could win,

Be laurelled, in order to sink, like Satan; you did;
I see this unmastery fight itself off now in me.
Twilight like a courtier bows at the long glass pane;

The Queen of Night allows access to her pavilion.
O, high sensation and archaic claims of style!
The tree that latticed our bodies with light and shade
When we wake is not a metaphor or natural—

Spoken into greenery by this thrill of penmanship—
Spendthrift and untidy on a foolscap before sleep.
Your adoration has slackened on the bed

And yet by force of habit are we both read
On one page forever unioned by a line's crown.
Such a coronation of an abstract love is
Grandiose perfection of the written ring.

Hammersmith, May 2009

After Terence Tiller

Spring at the Tropic of Cancer
Is not Spring in England.
The Arabian ocean is warm
As blood served in a bowl
While England's rain is cool.

Both Muscat and London swarm
With meaning for new lovers.
Old lovers make do with cold
In either hemisphere—
Fear in the water or on the sand
Is hope loosening hold of her hand.

On the Sublime

Green is the widest colour other than black which extends
Like an ocean, as far as the mind's hand; it is edible, lush,

Can be found in the iris, on scissor handles, ballpoint pens.
To leap your horse across the test, from Orion to Point X

Without felling steeples is a minor miracle, a major turn,
And suggests godlike prowess, the sinews of the angelic

Or years of practice in the heavens with atomic jodhpurs
Made of gold peeled from Midas as he slept cold dreams.

God has left us like a girl

(*after a line from Sidney Keyes*)

She has gone, out of the house
and down the stairs, her scent
evident and sweet as lilacs,
shaping her descent in the air,
leaving us alone to pray
that tomorrow, again, she will
deign to, lightly, reappear.

August 1982, Lac Bridgen

Last how memory won't come,
Late how the trick doesn't snap.
No click of it, some snag at back,
There's fur on the feathers,
Suntan on petals, rust in our soup.

It was hampering rain on the tin
Or ten ton hammering up the foil.
All the oil on the lake from engines
And loons honking out of season;
Boxes of Penguins; murder mostly.

Not to admit mice, but there they were,
Hopping beam to beam mad as veins.
Stone stabs the water with its white.
A black grave when the sun went off.
A lake is like a lid; it hides what it sees.
Can't locate lyricism in this head.

You have to remember to create.
What I write down is not only happening
It is making me realise what I have missed.

Seven Good Fridays

'Of love beyond desire, and so liberation'
—T.S. Eliot, from 'Little Gidding'

I.

April takes vinegar once a year—
Easter I turned forty, gave up youth
And reckless afternoons endowed with darkness—

Being twenty is like being a millionaire
About to be ruined in a house of sweat and roses—
Shadowed by near loss (premature,

Incubated, my parents cradling my smallness
To cherish the weak miracle guarded by glass)—
I should have come in to the world in summer

Not shadowing the saviour like a blinking twin
Upstaging his unbroken promise on the skull
With a spring birth, small, infertile.

II.

Tongue taking what's distributed,
It is time to observe a silence
And in that silence rise and sing.

III.

The mystery of words
Is a moment of intensity
Carved in time with words.

Day, after a night of tumult
And no repose; I sleep to cry out,
Bothering the bed with recollections.

My father, eyes craving health.
Embrace him. I try to heal but
My hands come away from the body

Wet with blood and faeces. Balm
Cannot secure a corpse from time.
I will begin to deceive the surgeon,

Borrow his steel into the bargain,
And relieve paternal wounds, winding
Words. I will apply a salve, to save.

IV.

Caution is not the dancer's way
With music, or the porpoise
Commanding vast water. To obey
Form is to occupy all wings

Of its theatre—flowing space
Across the stage, a sort of flung bouquet—
Mastery requires indifference,
Less majesty, more rude straying—

Indulge in what one loves, one wants,
Whether it be old or new, in one's gift
To give or merely taken on loan—
Indulge at last in a thrown saying.

V.

We moved to priapic Budapest.
In Montreal, Sara had mounted

A bicycle one late evening
On boulevard St Laurent—I followed

To Middle Europe, a wild card.
We were never lost among the ruins

We moved among, carried always
By the map of our selves, our shared

Aim to arrive safely, together, elsewhere.
We honeymooned on Hydra, island

Of laughter, but also bad dreams.
The accident offered our love

The quality of careful workmanship:
Hope is only as smart

As home is possible.
What is music but a scramble

For charmed time, a network
Of tintinnabulations made unfamiliar

In the sequenced air? A bumblebee
Will adumbrate, with élan, its fertile

Music, in a yellow field, upon
A family of ensunned flowers.

   VI.

You laughed that winter, as I placed
A gargantuan toque upon your head,
Crowning you queen of the white snow.

Now, that snow is gone, is clear
As the water that dried off Ararat,
The world cleansed or differently bled.

VII.

Words sustain the body
By being a kind
Of mouth for the spirit—

Unable to die completely,
Thereby living again,
When the stone

Is turned away
With the reading,
Communicating, eye.

My 43rd Year

History presses like a wall
against our shy backs—
shall we take the floor,
now that nothing costs more
than it did in 1944, and dance?
Life is such that one has to go
in and out of doors of great hotels
to sleep on beds that later are remade
while all the bills get paid
by an invisible millionaire
for some, while others become maids
or valets until their skin goes grey.
The sun will return in the morning

to remind us that the night belongs
to priest and demon equally,
and after the eighteenth-floor leap
into the delicate unspeaking air,
the chauffeurs look the other way.
I was sad before, and may be later today.
You and I pump blood and adore
the time we were given to love
but sense, like tiny clocks that must wake
prime ministers to greet mountains,
our time is soon, and the falls send up spray
so that we cling more closely, less lonely
in the battery and indiscipline of the fray.

St Peter and St Paul

At Mass the man behind me always coughs
So when we say peace and shake
There are germs between us
I rub off when I've left into the sun
Guilty for my suspicion
Why I am always ill is him
I am glad to be here among people
Who believe, or try to
God I haven't seen, local or abroad
After the death of my father
One September
A tree took on the affections
And silently impressed me
With the idea it might contain love
Beyond all measure
This I think of when I pray
Also, it needs to be understood
That most of the things asked for
Don't arrive
Bad post office, faith
Famine
And we eat out of hunger
I screw up my mind and try to recall
All the ones I want to see again or help
The prayers that rise to them are bubbles
Out of the mouths of fish
On the surface of things are barely visible
In childhood we catch kindness like the measles
And for some it stays
A habit that makes us care
Most are harder than that, having grown
Up into the evenly distributed air

I light a blue candle
For the young boy my brother and his wife have
Godson
He's never seen me, I live
Across the Atlantic in London
Multiple city of murder
And plays about murder
And commerce
These acts I do
In the absence of his knowing
As I do this now in the absence of knowledge
As to who hears, who ever listens
Love gets called for but may not be given
On earth or in heaven
There is always a spare pew
In front of the coughing man

Brook Green, London, 28 June 2009

October ray

Listening to Grand Pianola
Am a grand fellow
London October in the bones

X-raying nostalgia in
All yellowish leaves, blushes
Of trees, paltry as they please,

A thanksgiving; phones
Can't say hello to the buried;
Mellow the evening light dying.

This is the sound of not crying.
Planning to eat more this winter
And jog around the misty track

Crisp as a new pound in-pocket.
Aglow, little pumpkin guys
Brain-eaten by candlelight

Clambering in their headspace;
Dry-rot of the wet days of senses
Overburdening autumn's tumble;

Always love myself more in autumn;
Outside is resisting; is compositional;
Divide a score into seasons; each quarter

Year a quartet; reason to have a blessing;
Candle in shallow shadow, shut-in
Windowsill; pattering rain; meant

Emoting; sweetness as day dies.
Over the burning leaves hovers a scent
Of New England, oh its old youth scant yet

Ever-present, such pleasant smoke yearning;
In first England lies down the second one
As lines burn off their once-green in being lit.

Maida Vale, 1 October, 2010

On Television

We sat, without judgement, appearing
To look into what constantly appeared.
Why is it so disgraceful
To be transported and amused
By the unseen energies of a fuse?
How these pictures lift and land
Across the room, noble as a plane,
Lit, active, flashing, grand;
Thrown like a magician's bird
Out of the black hat of its box.
The rain outside, the screen sun
Warm as a holiday, your hand
Half-open for mine, endazed,
As unreality spun and blazed.

New Country

Declaring the flag, they flew
Across valleys, flinging shots
Like shouts, off stone ministries
Swelling to a nation in some streets;
Insolent crayons in bluster's fist—
Identities scrawled, blood-by-ink,
Each declaration, an equal foe
Not wanting to have heard it—
Lands are chastised, though, taken
Back to day one, then some, predawn.
Light is always violent expansion.

Song In A Time of Inflation

Only you, and money, and sunlight
Hold up any clear possibility,

And joy is not to be undervalued,
Is to be portfolio-carried, a fluid

Securitisation, to transfer one kind
Of happiness across to another form;

Words are only digital on a screen,
In one account or another

There's a vault holding all our hearts,
Our souls, our meanings.

Westerners are better than the others,
More perfectly formed, more joyous,

Handsome and wearing watches
Meant to be passed down father to son;

My plane lands at noon, cars speed
To collect us, your long smart legs

Slip out of the vehicle, onto the tarmac.
At the UN we trade tongues like critics

To hold some sort of pretty balance.
If we smile and agree, we are good;

If we frown and snarl, we are foreign.
However, we love to make love to women

Who are dressed in Paris, and address
Large forums. No lions roar

In the mountains anymore, they run
Riot, on goldleaf paws, among the City.

I want you; you do not know me
Since I am blacked out, a face speaking

On an interview in Dangerzone Three.
Green as the citadels are, clusters

Of eruption upset the lyric of promise,
Love comes buzzing lies like malaria

Shifts and shudders on a sweaty sheet,
Like desire to be posthumous writes

Words into the stream of any body.
Our fuel's costly, my jet's coming soon.

Vroom and clutch, swoon and dance—
It's sunny in host veins and currency

Urgently insists we all have a reason
To create offspring, to congregate here

In the sweet summer gardens of fear,
In fearsome gardens of sweet summer.

Shop-Worn

Age sells to youth
So many things it will come to regret;

But not yet—ah no, not yet.
For now, youth buys and buys,

From old hands, lies made new,
Puts them on and turns

To show its mirror how to learn
How wearing beauty lets

It be true—if only
For a season, then with rue.

The Farmer's Wife

was taken to a far-off hospital then nothing was born. Stood
seeing a clock do its rounds. Seen animals suffering this way.
After three days, left to keep the world of small hours going.

She stayed, child-prolonged. Doctors promised to send word
when one of two promises life holds (one in either hand) opened:
to come into light or go from it. Felt her heaviness, going about

regular work: how she in-carried a future. News arrived late.
Police car blinking in the dawn. The pail of feed ungrasped,
body leaning, a hangman's noose around the throat. *Daughter.*

Azoospermia

In the late summer I saw my future.
Not gaudy, hardly mine,
Brought to me by a blunt test.
The trees were alert to the wind.
Parents threw their dismal joy
And busy disorder about
The streets. The park strained
At its collar, barked with playing;
The hours in my head abruptly
Stuck. Now I was sterile.
All my weird kids blinked out
UFOS off the radar—
In a moment that stayed around
Like an invasion long planned,
That held its breath, that froze
My bones to my mouth—
I tasted the invisible loss
Of hopes going out. Maudlin,
So private, but pain occurs
Even when the reason's sentimental.
I attempted profound respect
For nature. Nodded sagely
At my secret body's amazing failure.
Considered new identities—
A renewed gender. Freed
From the requirement to breed,
I momentarily thrilled at time,
Now heaped, big, before me—
No Daddy-wasting anymore—
I'd learn Chinese, particle physics—
Hard to be ordinary when rare—
Free from expecting anything—

I gave my wife the gift of nothing—
I planted autumn in our garden—
I put a small stone in the basin—
I placed black glass on our bed—
I laid us down on sand and turned
Away. I walked around, around
The streets here, radiating inexistence—
My name meant never-been—was-not—
I came bringing no warriors in the horse—
All those dumbly-wasted Trojans—
My fate a silly-sounding freak
Of a word—(not even one dead one!)—
Empty as a collection plate before communion.

After riding the escalator back

to switch the watch
a Swatch a second time, a third,
each face scratched minutely,

or because the date was stuck
I became a traveller in the mall
forever unhappy with a purchase

but returning always unalone
brought there with my wife
who loves me and worries for

the sorrow that ticks away
inside the case of my self-schism
but that's not all

I go up and offer each broken
or semi-imperfect object to
the kindly merchant of watches

who resembles a small Paul Simon
which is smaller than you might
imagine possible, and while

outside there is London getting
Sunday under a darkening wing
inside it is the timelessness

of some brief caring act,
not entirely due to exchange of
money, and I am in love

and ruined in some parts of inner
workings, a cog that clicks
upon another toothed gear

stymied again, under the magnifying
glass, still unable to be pried free—
sorrow's just an hour by hour

journey, but in between, there are
seconds as good as before, pretty
good intervals to cling to you and me.

When all my disappointments came at once

I greeted them as guests,
brought them in and settled their burdens
with footstools, olives and cool white wine.

This was a delicate stage—
they'd never met in one room before—
had circled warily in the past, strangers

to themselves if not to me (for I
had often expected, if not them,
others with equal claim on my time).

Now, none of my hospitality paid off
for they began to quarrel
over who would take my will to go on

first—each wanted to be the foremost cause
of my early failure to stay living.
Frames came off nails; books spilled; lights

fell like building blocks; stains spread.
During their intensity of competition
I took off over the garden wall, refreshed.

Fertility

Bolts past, and past, and through names.
History seems young beside its fluent flame—
The rootless flower, the star without a start—
The reason for being early, or late,
The richest date, the opposite of zero,
The cognate's cognate, the king's bee,
The blackness of blackness being reversed,
The hero who sits up and laughs in the hearse;
The only manner in which death is cursed;
The stage on which all monkeys rehearse Lear;
The queer split shiver erupting ingots across
Time so bars of body and knowing solidify
To be born; it is the spliced film of things,
The jumpsuit, the steamboat's toot, the lute
That strings of numbers explode sideways into.
Without this fractious miracle, this intervention
No one, no mind, no skin, no lips, no eye, no one;
How the spill slip causeway goes against caution;
It outdoes eloquence, requires no passion.
Can there be such control in the spasm of the sea,
Such science in the lightning strike that crosses Z
With A, dashing across all letters, chromosome by
Chromosome, unzipping, sped by dot and hyphen,
So real it makes accidents of each, women, men,
Makes love sometimes a field of gold intention,
Waves of tousled, febrile, sweet information?
Its shadow is arctic nullity, the barren place
Where loss is chaste, and memory is not
Chased, across a tundra of insufficiency.
Not to be the fire but the water that shuts off fire;
Each body carrying a coin that turns on life or not;
Parenting or oblivion; to prosper or be forgotten.

Sonnet

No children;
Cold uncoils in the blood;
Science, true, not good
For you. So old,
Suddenly, or so young.
Lyric inside not to be sung.
Plug pulled, screen gone.
Sun out; mind
Bountiful, playing pain.
These are my children
In my head. Unbegotten.
This is to self-forget,
To have the future
Born forgotten.

Our Children

Love has the power to undo
nothing, but like a refrain, returns
to that absence so often
it becomes a thing, a lake of fire

in which husband and wife
bathe when going to bed
and when rising in the morning
to the rooms of the lit dark house.

St Lambert

A specific loneliness
Saying nothing

Across a field
Behind the low school

Snow on the track
Child, or childless man—

The time it took
To remember this

The Runner

I saw you on the track
In your violent yellow
Small as an eye, rounding

The track, the only circuit
Of any value to me now.
Don't stop, small runner.

You embody loving.
Should you cease to run,
Be stopped, I would stop too.

Slieve Donard

The sea and the hotel
are dull and plentiful
like time in hospital.
Guests from windows
read books on Mahler

then look down on waves
seriously grey, possibly
ruinous or deadly.
White as healed scars,
a sea sub-zero in style.

Long women in furs
stroll glamour along
the beach, thinking
of Charlie Chaplin
who stayed there once

as did Percy French
who preferred the Mourne
mountains slumping
to the water, to London's
gold-flecked streets,

its lips rose-tinted.
The sun, a film actor
in a suite, fails to make
an appearance on the scene.
The hidden horizon

is modern in its abstractions:
fog-within-fog, as light

flattens into a Prussian
afternoon—austere silence
slowly rising to the ledge

lapping hotel, sea, guest and sky
in sadness, a chill that feels
symbolic, that cries out
*look on birth and death
as equal ships passing*

out past gnashing rocks!—
ships lit to some distant passage
by a faint lighthouse
a comic smudge of hope
pressed like an insect

into the book of night.
Then, the lamps and beams
snap on, casting the place
into immaculate grandeur
on its ambiguous lawn—tight

by wild sea and high summit—
as a bald man gazes in the spa
out on a dark car park
sometimes bothered by a car
and Magda brings tea to a couple

come to the resort to mourn
their inability to conceive
even by acts of love.
Tall curtains are pulled.
The tide turns. The sky thickens.

'Down from St John's Wood'

Down from St John's Wood hospital
The sun allows the promenade
I undertake, foiling dark fear
That what resides within my body

Is soon to tear. The leaves are weak,
Unsettle and disappear. The day
Is a Tartuffe of weather: a face
Of gold that may say other things

Elsewhere; the old fact, under a counter
Lies a gun, a bat. The world
Is not just mansions and private security
Though that part is real and looks good;

Inside the perimeters we guard
An unidentifiable aspect like a name;
A pulse or compulsion to think as light;
A presence that flames, gutters, flames;

A soul or mind or intangible perforation.
This beyond-words-shade is all I speak,
Flings me to Maida Vale for a vacation,
A lessening, needed, to coronate

That part alluded to, which, compressed,
Thins out, beaten, to a leaf that breaks;
Snapped in the sway of emotionality,
A wavelike battering of the interior.

September 2009

September's End

Some weeks I walk in autumn in mentality.
It burns like a St Lambert girl's red hair—
Bursts through curtains, sun-knife in air.
Though a golden thing is going, I am calm.
I keep calm, though the remaining trees
Are anxious to be broken, as strings
Untidily, colour going to the bank

To be cleaned—a totally empty bank:
Rivers of money spawn leaping drought.
All about is quantity, lush ownership
Tossed aside—we're haughty on a date
By a boy's side we had not fancied overly—
Only wanting attention's silly powers.
I am calm, if sad, to stroll hereabouts now.

Hope, Maida Vale

Purcell in the room,
December exterior to glass,
beyond the white radiator's coils
I watch the athletes, floodlit,
and also enjoy aspects of the park
more wintry and more dark.

Fell into summer gloom
lasted longer, wouldn't pass;
it came to be my work, but toils
of a sad kind; a bad toolkit
knocking at my soul. No spark.
Now vague singing. A bare lark.

Even as you are wrapped for a tomb
hope to see light running out of dark.

December 2009

Near St Ives

Upon the sand the lifeguard goes
To lift his flag (yellow and red)
And advance it closer to the dunes,
As a slow rush of tide idealises
The duty, makes its purpose real.

Watching the lone figure walking there
In the noon mist, the windsock's flare
Warning not to float upon the waves,
The loneliness of waiting to be useful saves
Each one of us from our given landscape,

Or the slimmest task. An hour later,
Above Porthkidney on the coastal path
To St Ives, the beige has been submerged;
The clean green water has moved in—
The flags gone, no bathers to protect;

As if crossing the Sahara to me, a mirage,
I hold the image of the red-dressed man,
Stooped under the billowing standard of his select
Role—to be present on an empty beach, lest
Even one soul find difficulty in water;

And such flags as fly to say a person's careful
With another's delight comforts my otherwise
Dubious mind; aftermath of loss
Resolves itself to chores of kindness
Along shores where light settles, enhances.

Fire Killed The Sculptor As She Worked

You read *Twilight* twice, as if loving vampires
Provided a different way to extend a bloodline.

I'd watch you tearing through those paperbacks
Marvelling at your ability to be deceived

By craft. Meanwhile, I suffered setbacks.
One can become a connoisseur of anything,

Even antibiotics. Our reprieve was St Ives.
Hepworth's garden in light rain combined a jungle

With cold modernism—a horizon we admired.
Her fire-wrecked atelier. Nude loss reclining.

The Snow Child

Then, it being winter, snow came.
The schools and the banks ended
As if in tales where all came good.

Our garden was turned abruptly
Into an enchanted wood, white white
So we went out like children

To make a personal figure in the cold
With our own hands. You rolled the balls
Of the body. I brought out the carrot,

Gathered twigs for limbs. We built our child
With conscious caution, too engrossed
In making what we could of nature.

Then stood back to admire the human look
Of our pitiful creation. Pitiful because
The small thing was composed of ice

And would fail to last, or learn
Or go on being ours for long;
By morning, trampled down—

Particles, bits and chunks, a rumour
Of what it had been to us: a snow-child
Killed by real kids, cruel to snow as rain.

Slieve Donard II

The suite on the side
facing away from the sea
is the suite with the fireplace
and two plasma-screen TVs.
Better luxury compensates
for lack of view. Before
the perpetual gas fire, stunned
as if into stone, entering

as you enter your Anne Brontë
a world muted, chemically arranged,
I try renewal of a mind remade.
Mind is book is water is fire, all change.
Fear is the wake-up call at three,
too early for planes. Airport quiet.
Leave the hotel without baggage, fly
direct to Geneva. They await you there.

What occurs is only the turning of a page,
imagined for screen. Unseen is greater.
Is attested to, as we rise in Mass.
Water should be avoided by all those
who get into difficulty with ease, and cats.
Searching for the BlackBerry in the fur-lined
coat, I roam and ring, opening
a closet, from which tumbles a victim,

providing a fitting climax. Mrs. Pontifax
is staying across the hall. The glamour.
She is the Minister of Finance's daughter.
She sees the cold winter sea rise from her vantage.
Our age is blinded by celebrity, seeing

with the gilded orb of a bronze, dull god.
The domes of our room service cool
after we have slaked and fed. As you read

this becomes the first one written under the influence
of an anti-depressed self, whatever that is to be.
What is, is taken off a shelf, a remaining wrack
that half emerges from the brackish ruins of the year.
Will love reunite?
Will Ireland be solvent?
All nights, holiest, least holy,
be still, be silent.

Ireland, Christmas, 2009

A Walk With Sara In September

In Hammersmith Grove
We walked for love.
Alone it felt, though a moon
Presented most of itself above

The small tidied houses
In their silent rows: graves
It looked, for no one moved
Except one deaf man we met

Who did not hear us
Wish him well, but passed
Into his gate. And a fox
We chased down the middle

Of the street. We came and went
In the moonlight like spirits
Or guards, able to go as we pleased,
Turned this way and that

As small curved road
After little lane appeared, all silent.
Sometimes our hands held;
Other times, as we feared less,

They broke apart. When you ran
To a dead end and saw
A star cross the sky falling,
I asked you to say a wish,

Which you did, but confessed
Later not for what I'd hoped for.
My illness had kept me enclosed,
This openness was good:

To walk with my dear wife
In a place subtle as a wood.

Old Master

I was very lovely then, fragile,
Bone china, a fine line, a tree
Telling time to be pretty; in love—

The young came to my shop, contoured
In ways that remind desire to break
Open; as spring does; as do flames.

Their names have disappeared—did they
Have any? Their shapes are here
Pressed within a range of cold materials.

Improbable August

Thrown off course by being back
TGV-forward to Avignon.
France replaces England

Effortlessly in these my affections.
Dull sun powders the fields
Whose wheat's been boxed.

A dull sun but still it burns
Away seven years of cold
In one careless touch. Suns

Could care less what farms
Produce, when leaves flare
Under their vast informing sway.

My world brushes up against froideur
But turns also to glow in a sunflower
That like casual or first-seen love rides

On night's coulds and might-have-beens
As desire's object leans just so, just there.
Glad fitfully to be alivened on loan

Let off by despair, I let later light
Brush my hair, burnish my bronze hours
To a nuanced golden throne aloft on lack.

Pont D'Avignon

I think the wind could throw children
To their wet slaughter if it tried.

So limited these railings—the snub-nose
Of the thing just starts where stone stops—
A sloping blunt snap then air—

Built to show where the dead go
When overburdened angels shrug them off.

Winter Storm Lothar

A winter storm budged the lid,
Thieving a tree on which we'd carved
Two names, a dove, a crown.
The force of it

Stove in the steeple
Displaced three cars
Across the newly-risen rectory
Lawn, desecrating love,

Or the growing
Symbol we had both picked
To hold it in
Place. Sly Lothar, another lover

Spied, from far above, your arms
Cradling my cries—turned
Wide in envy's circle. Then
The whole sky was torn in two.

The Safe Years

The safe years are behind us now,
So prepare for what will come to us
She said, and the wind
Blew sage brush and ash
Around our table, where
A woman with red lipstick
Served green tea—the room
Moved to another room,
Time became Augustinian,
Difficult, and rough-hewn,
Feeling emotional, as it would—
We have no way to exist after dying—
Fame or memory are only conceits—
The years advance, and decline as one—
As paddles raised to tell pilots to fly
Then drop down with the same arm—
And Seneca took his own life;
Kings wanted sons; wanted a line—
No lines supply the ones behind enemy
Lines—which is where all bodies are—
Yes, man and woman dining in the café,
You are fighting, not with each other,
Not, as you think, because of infertility,
Those fears and lost things, little dreams,
Fripperies that perform the shape of hoping
(We fumble about with little dreams
Of simple things, like baby showers,
Graduation gowns; arms flung to say Mom,
Dad)—you're fighting with the body itself,
With some mechanical decision made, as if
By accident, but rational no doubt,
Something genetic, some blockage, a

Clicking off or on of some chemistry
That means your plane will not land—
It started on a fine day, blown apart—
Your heart like a storm blows up from
A fine day, will go on over the desert,
Until it ceases, and you and your wife
Are buried together, childless, collected:
Calm in love's entire silence, entire end.

For Sara

My heart leapt like a fool
thinking to see you come to my door

as it capered gaily once before
that otherwise distant Yule

when all the flowers known
to man burst from your proffering

as I opened out to your windblown
dignity and felt the dumbness sing.

November 2009

Start again

In a key of slow
Then again stop and go.
Are trees made of pianos
Or the other way?

March plays the bare bones
Like it was evening
In a dive, solo.
Beneath the poverty

A billionaire lies
Domiciled in the soil
And about to pay out glowing
Light and growth.

Recover is what the ill
Try to do, and succeed
Or die. Health is a portfolio
We all want into.

I am putting these together
Not as if my life depended
On the assembly, that's bomb
Disposal. Or disassembly,

Critical. Wires cross
As leaves revive cool green
And April steps out
Into the sun after a year

On the town, run down, has-been.
Nothing cyclical gets lost:
Time spins and so is redeemed;
Spins because planetary, so

Laws define the poetic sense
That hope is eternal; poetry
Makes lawyers of us all.
I step forward knowing my foot

Slips as part of its patter,
Faster then slower, not always
A goer but ready for a tip or jot.
No longer hot toddy, I warm

To the idea of writing
As a second chance to fail.
The grandeur was always second-hand,
Beauty the accident in what we planned;

The birth of someone else's child
When your hallway has no pram.
Gutted is the direction we head in
Leaving traces of our loss behind—

A fish dragged across the water
On a line you'd miss until blind.
I felt loss when it left me
Saw what I had as it flew

Caught the train by jumping ship
And sailed for home in a caboose
Boxed my eagles with an iron glove
Glued love to my ears, loose but true.

Lines Composed On The Poet's Sterility

Had I my druthers, would have fathered
A whole family freely, fully,
Been fecund. But history has its moons
On which nothing is, and endlessly.
This moon risen in my loins ices
Flowering so even potential nature
Becomes (uncomes) artifice.
Now to land on a surface lacking life
Is airless drag, but imagination supplies
Colonies, domes visions, rocket families placid
Against the glass, faces to the blue sweetness.

Hunting Party

A heart is sacred, a wounded hart;
Outrun the symbol in the wood.

Pluck out the arrows. The head
Enters after having been shot through

The air, in order to hunt and halt
The glorious animal that will be eaten;

Flesh parts from pelt; horns rise on walls.
The hall hums with music's knowing.

This is the festival in the glade,
The pump-pump of the love brigade,

That process known as seasonal,
The turn from rose to worm, grass to spade.

After a First Line by David Lehman

What is the purpose of your poems?
Not to be outdone
By any squadron or bazillionaire.
To rise like air, to fool Miss Marple.

To haunt the pale beauty in the silver ghost.
To compete with trophy or martini;
To be longer than infinity.
In short, to be better than normal words

Stamped onto boards to sell on sale.
Bread and words go stale.
To outbrilliant the sun.
To fail completely. To sail to China

And be back in time to boil green tea.
To have no plan. To set questions on fire.
To halt desire by outstaying calm.
To taste the tip of tiger balm.

To tie up you and me
Sweetly but with dexterity.
To spread out the lovely cherry trees
Up and down the mourning town.

Esophagitis

I have walked out to you
And met in lamplight and been
Placed so well in joyous peace.

Those walks under the trees
Are the past that matters to me,
Upon which I am based. Because

Of early incidents I only sought love,
And, finding it in you, ceased
To need what else the world offers

Or retracts. These days are difficult.
The bitter acid in my throat is actual.
I burn down to what cannot speak or heal.

Receding from happy climate to despair
Means a change of air; less
And gasping, I choke. How to place

The joy in this new context of painful fear?
That year is not this year. That love where?
Prayer: could it make us walk back there.

Love Or Poetry

I know now that love, not poetry, will save me
From your blessed injuries, your uneven surfaces,

Like a line that doesn't work. It won't open out
Like love will. Poetry mutters, scuttles, rebuts.

I strut now in bars of sure sheer sun, unashamed
Of my lack of poetry. I swoon to swim in prose.

I love what this lack of tortured syntax means;
It means I can go waste my life being ordinary.

London Reflux

The surprising stillness
of the antidepressant
holds back my art
but not my regret.

Snow settles, as do minds.
Pull down these blinds.
Midway through
forty-three I became eighty-six.

That clumsy age. I dropped
a lot of tricks and poses.
Responsibilities like marbles
trip-wired my new-tiled floor.

I showed my job the door.
Kicked health downstairs.
I have it, a bit,
can squint my mind

to see a word target.
I know what's around corners,
even if I stay put, mainly.
A burnt windpipe leads to self-pity.

The self was devised that way.
Lick the wound of the self by yourself.
See what raw red mess you made.
Around an edge of haze, roses.

19 November, 2009

Rain

Rain comforts with its hands, sends
Walkers running, runners to stand
Still beneath doors and shops
Never stopped at before.

Yet, cold from heaven
Has warmth, sets a hearth up:
Blackens the ground, whets green
To be its sharp kind. Sounds a mind.

Water in a Lakeland Vale

White water white water
Running out like a daughter

Like a son onto green grass
Gray stone white water

Across across down down
Water comes to shift expand

Undoing the mountain
Bending down as it goes

What's spoken is spackled
What's shifted is on show

Request

Stay, lie with me when I die
and keep me now I am dead.

Married as the sun is warm
let your arm maintain my head.

Move here beside cold love,
while my new body is identified,

different from what living is.
Hold me on what was our bed.

Fold your arms around what stays
when older forms of love have fled.

The Ailment

What got there, got there
then it stayed. *Like glue*
a doctor implied. *Like prayer*
argued another clad like a father
black as grease. It stung
and stuck inside. *A thorn*

she cried; *a hornet having died*
the priest complained—*unsin
thy side!* It was presented
in a finding so I had to decide:
*pull out the fervid pin or wasp
away to little else besides lather*

on a shaved boy's chin. Its clasp
was like wax on a ski or an LP's skin.
It slid about, it grooved, it played
the length and lines of me, a musicness
unto breath. *A tiny ceaseless death*
the dentist opined then wanted cash.

It felt like wine-slosh in my brainpan.
All night I travelled in my bed, a train.
Each carriage disgorged an ailment
but this main thing only grew in size.
It happened finally to emit a claim
on my own name. It wanted out

but as me. I feigned indifference
to my external self, retained some
dignity. Soon though, unguents came
and took the resourceful fluid for a stroll.
It shook off the air and walked upright, so
everyone who saw it nodded at *my soul.*

Author Biography

Todd Swift is a Canadian poet whose work has appeared in many major publications, including *Poetry* (Chicago), *Poetry Review*, and *The Globe and Mail*. He is author of seven previous poetry collections, most recently *England Is Mine* (DC Books) and has edited or co-edited numerous popular anthologies, including *Modern Canadian Poets* (Carcanet, 2010), and *Lung Jazz: Young British Poets for Oxfam* (Cinnamon, 2012). He was Oxfam GB Poet-in-residence in 2004. He has a PHD in Creative and Critical Writing from the University of East Anglia (UEA), and lectures in creative writing at Kingston University, in England. He lives in Maida Vale, London, with his Irish wife Sara.

Author Photo by Derek Adams

Acknowledgements

Earlier versions of these poems first appeared in the following online and print publications; a grateful thank you to their publishers is here offered.

'The Shelf' in *Seaway* (Ireland).
'On Reading Martin Mooney' in *Molossus* (India).
'Michael Kohlhaas' in *The Ugly Tree* (UK).
'Hedda Gabler' in *Upstairs At Duroc* (France).
'Amirs of the House of Rashid' in *Molossus* (India).
'I think of Delmore Schwartz beside my sleeping love' in
    Blackbox Manifold (UK).
'God Has Left Us Like A Girl' in *Mainstream Love Hotel* (UK).
'August 1982, Lac Brigden' on NationalPoetryMonth.ca
    (April 2012).
'My 43rd year' in the e-pamphlet The Awards Ceremony from
    Silkwords Inc (UK).
'Song In A Time of Inflation' in *Mainstream Love Hotel* (UK).
'Azoospermia' in *Gargoyle* (USA).
'After Riding The Escalator Back' in *Canadian Literature*.
'When all my disappointments came at once' in *Hand + Star* (UK).
'Fertility' in *Seaway* (Ireland).
'Sonnet' in *Poetry* (Chicago, USA).
'St Lambert' in *The Stinging Fly* (Ireland).
'Slieve Donard' in *Poetry Review* (UK).
'Down From St John's Wood' in *Molossus* (India).
'September's End' in *Molossus* (India)
'Near St Ives' in *Molossus* (India).
'Slieve Donard II' in *Poetry* (Chicago, USA).
'Old Master' in *Horizon Review* (UK).
'Improbable August' in *Peony Moon* (South Africa).
'Pont D'Avignon' in *Freefall*.
'The Safe Years' in *The Moth* (Ireland).
'Winter Storm Lothar' in *Atlas* (India).

'Start Again' in the e-pamphlet The Awards Ceremony from *Silkwords Inc* (UK).
'Hunting Party' in *Horizon Review* (UK).
'Love Or Poetry' in *Peony Moon* (South Africa).
'Request' in *Other Lives* (UK).

The poems in this collection were mostly written during a fraught time; and many were first written for my PHD thesis at the University of East Anglia, under the expert supervision of Professors Denise Riley and Jon Cook, without whom this work would not have been completed in such a manner. Catherine Graham edited the poems subtly and sensitively. I am very grateful to Stewart MacFarlane for the kind donation of his brilliant art work.

A few other people were especially helpful and supportive during this time, working with me on these poems, or in other equally invaluable, sometimes medical or personal, capacities, and I would like to thank them here: Al Alvarez, Alex McRae, Ann Egan, Bridget Hourican, Clive Scott, David Lehman, David Rogers, Diana Bryden, Don Share, Dr. E. Sass, Dr. Jennifer Gomborone, Dr. Richard Marley, Emily Berry, Fiona Sampson, Fr. Oliver Brennan, Giles Goodland, Kevin Higgins, Ian Brinton, Ilya Kaminsky, James Byrne, Jason Camlot, Jeremy Noel-Tod, Jessie Lendennie, Jordan Swift, Les Robinson, Luke Kennard, Mark Ford, Martin Penny, Patrick Chapman, Phillip Gross, Professor Gerald Libby Sandeep Parmar, Sara Upstone, Sheila Hillier, Susan Briscoe, Wendy Cope, and Zoë Brigley.

Finally, let me thank other friends, fellow poets, and family members (they know who they are) who have been there for me. No one has been more loving or supportive than my beloved Sara, who has given me what poetry I have in my life, for years.

Praise for Todd Swift

"Poetry that's too self-consciously smart may leave one cold. We want feeling; we want to believe that a poet sees life wholly and loves it fiercely. We want to know that he or she faces the dilemma of our existence—a temporary sentience before oblivion (save for, perhaps, spiritual transcendence that we can only obtain through faith). Todd Swift is such a poet. His voice is powerfully his own, but poetry lovers will find the grace notes of plainsong T.S. Eliot, but also the verbal dexterity of Swift's fine compatriot, Robert Bringhurst. But what's most important is what Swift says to us about living—in words that are indelible because they are written in the heart's blood. Swift is a philosophical poet, a metaphysical poet, but he is also a poet of truths that he shows us anew. He knows that "Desire ages, ages hardly at all," and that it can "break / Open; as spring does; as do flames." Desire Swift; you'll have no disappointment. This collection is compassion in mind, excellence in art."

—George Elliott Clarke, Laureate, 2001 Governor-General's Award for Poetry

"These thoughtful introspects marry the most difficult topics to make new—love, illness—with a contemporary sensibility. Swift is a descendent of Auden, and some of his lyric moments are joyously Audenesque. Often, though, there's a subtly decadent note: roses and wounds recur alongside the tender avowals. Importantly, the book's frank exploration of mid-life crisis is unusual, highly characteristic—and brave."

—Fiona Sampson, poet and 2005-2012 editor of *Poetry Review*

"This is a timely and important addition to Todd Swift's increasingly impressive body of work as a poet. One of contemporary English language poetry's great cosmopolitans, Swift takes the whole world for his subject. His words have a rare, and very particular, musicality. Almost every poem here has at least one line which I'm jealous I didn't write myself."
—Kevin Higgins, Irish poet

"This is a book full of difficult things—difficult knowledge, difficult experience—and yet its effect is strangely redemptive. I think this has something to do with a slow-motion exuberance in the writing itself—the almost Jacobean richness of the diction, the surprising and graceful turns of the syntax."
—Bill Manhire, winner of the New Zealand Book Award for poetry, and New Zealand's inaugural Poet Laureate

"These poems think their way through a difficult passage in the writer's life, without self indulgence or self pity. Not afraid to be literary, they show how conversations with the work of other writers and the disciplines of form can bring us through to moments of surprising grace."
—Philip Gross, winner of the T.S. Eliot Prize